How to Use This Book

A Variety of Presentations

1. Make overhead transparencies of the lessons. Present each lesso̶ ̶ ̶ ̶ ̶ ̶ ̶ , with the entire class. Write answers and make corrections using an erasab̶ ̶ ̶ ̶ ̶ ̶ ̶.

   As the class becomes more familiar with *Daily Word Problems,* have students mark their answers first and then check them against correct responses marked on the transparency.

2. Reproduce the problems for individuals or partners to work on independently. Check answers as a group, using an overhead transparency to model the solutions' strategies. (Use these pages as independent practice only after much group experience with the lessons.)

3. Occasionally you may want to reproduce problems as a test to see how individuals are progressing in their acquisition of skills.

Important Considerations

1. Allow students to use whatever tools they need to solve problems. Some students will choose to use manipulatives, while others will want to make drawings.

2. It is important that students share their solutions. Modeling a variety of problem-solving techniques makes students aware that there are different paths to the correct answer. Don't scrimp on the amount of time allowed for discussing how solutions were reached.

3. Teach students to follow problem-solving strategies:
   • Read the problem carefully more than one time. Think about it as you read.
   • Mark the important information in the problem.
        What question does the problem ask?
        What words will help you know how to solve the problem (*in all, left, how many more,* etc.)?
        What facts will help you answer the question? (Cross out facts that are NOT needed.)
   • Think about what you need to do to solve the problem (add, subtract, multiply, or divide).
   • Solve the problem. Does your answer make sense?
   • Check your answer.

Matrix Logic Puzzle

The Friday problem for week 19 is a matrix logic puzzle. Here are some guidelines for helping students solve this type of logic puzzle:

   • Read all the clues. Find clues that give a definite *Yes* or *No.* (For example: John plays the clarinet. Sally does not play the flute.) Mark boxes with X (for no) or **Yes**.
   • When you mark a box **Yes**, mark Xs in all the other boxes in that row and in the column above and below the X.
   • Find clues that give information, but not enough to tell you how to mark the boxes. Make notes in the boxes for later use.
   • Go over each clue again. Look for clues that fit together to give enough information to make a box **Yes** or **No**.

Scope and Sequence—Grade 3

Week	1	2	3	4	5	6	7	8	9	10	11	12	13	14	15	16	17	18	19	20	21	22	23	24	25	26	27	28	29	30	31	32	33	34	35	36
Addition Facts	•																		•																	
Subtraction Facts									•																											
Column Addition			•			•		•						•	•																		•			
Multiplication Facts (products to 25)			•				•			•				•																	•		•			
Division Facts (dividends to 25)	•	•		•																	•															
Multiplication Facts (products to 81)	•		•			•	•												•								•	•							•	
Division Facts (dividends to 81)					•																													•		
Multi-Digit Addition & Subtraction Without Regrouping		•		•								•			•								•			•							•	•		
Multi-Digit Addition & Subtraction With Regrouping				•	•		•	•		•			•	•		•		•				•	•		•	•	•	•	•		•	•	•	•	•	•
Multiplication Without Regrouping		•					•				•						•			•				•			•						•			
Multiplication With Regrouping							•						•									•		•	•			•	•		•			•		
Division Without Remainders											•		•					•							•											
Division With Remainders												•													•											
Fractions									•	•							•				•									•						
Time			•	•	•			•		•					•							•		•		•		•	•	•		•	•	•		
Money			•	•	•	•	•				•	•				•	•				•			•		•	•	•	•				•	•	•	
Units of Measurement											•	•																•		•						
Weight & Capacity												•										•														
Interpreting Graphs & Tables										•							•						•			•			•			•			•	
Data/Probability			•												•	•								•									•	•		
Geometry								•																	•		•									
Logic Problems											•					•	•		•						•						•					
Patterns							•																													•

Daily Word Problems • EMC 3003

Daily Word Problems

Monday-Week 1

Candles

Mindy's candle is 5 inches long. Her candle takes 10 minutes to burn 1 inch. How long will her candle burn?

Name:

Work Space:

$10 \times 5 = 50$ minutes

Answer:

_____50_____ minutes

Daily Word Problems

Tuesday-Week 1

Candles

Elisa is making candles. She needs 5 ounces of wax for each candle. She has 25 ounces of wax. How many candles can she make?

Name:

Work Space:

$\begin{array}{r} 25 \\ \div\ 5 \\ \hline 5 \text{ candles} \end{array}$

Answer:

_____5_____ candles

Daily Word Problems

Wednesday-Week 1

Candles

It's Ian's birthday. He is 10 years old. How many candles has Ian had on all of his birthday cakes? Remember, he has had 10 birthday cakes.

Name:

Work Space:

1+2+3+4+5+6+7+8+9+10
=55 candles

Answer:

_55_ candles

Daily Word Problems

Thursday-Week 1

Candles

Elisa is making candles. She knows each candle needs a wick that is 4 inches long. She wants to make 7 candles. How many inches of wick will she need?

Name:

Work Space:

7×4=28 wick
inch of wick

Answer:

_28_ inches of wick

Daily Word Problems

Friday-Week 1

Candles

Welcome to Make Your Own Candle Store. You have 3 candles to decorate. Use all the decorations listed below. Each candle must have the same number of each decoration.

- 6 smiling faces
- 9 stars
- 3 bows
- 12 flowers

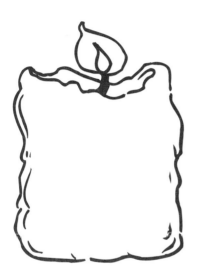  

Use the candles you decorated to answer the following questions.

- How many smiling faces are on each of the candles? _____

- How many stars are on each of the candles? _____

- How many bows are on each of the candles? _____

- How many flowers are on each of the candles? _____

- How did you find the number of each decoration for each candle?

_____

_____

5

Daily Word Problems

Monday–Week 2

School Bus

Jan gets on the school bus at 8:15 a.m. She rides the bus for 35 minutes. At what time does Jan arrive at school?

Name:

Work Space:

Answer:

_____ : _____

Daily Word Problems

Tuesday–Week 2

School Bus

The school bus has 14 seats. Two students can sit on each seat. If all the seats on the bus are full, how many students are riding the bus?

Name:

Work Space:

Answer:

_____ students

Daily Word Problems

Wednesday-Week 2

School Bus

There are 28 students riding the bus. Twelve of the students are girls. How many boys are riding the bus?

Name:

Work Space:

Answer:

_____ boys

Daily Word Problems

Thursday-Week 2

School Bus

The school bus travels 5 miles on one gallon of gas. How many gallons of gas will the bus use on its 20-mile route?

Name:

Work Space:

Answer:

_____ gallons

Daily Word Problems

Name: _____

School Bus

Use the chart to answer the questions below.

Students Riding the School Bus

Bus Stop	Number of Students
1	5
2	8
3	3
4	4
5	7
6	2

- How many **total** students get on the school bus? _____

- Which bus stop has the **most** students? _____

- Which bus stop has the **fewest** students? _____

- Which bus stop has **twice** as many students as bus stop 4? _____

- Which bus stop has **4 times** as many students as bus stop 6? _____

- Which bus stops have an **even** number of students? _____

- Which bus stops have an **odd** number of students? _____

Daily Word Problems

Monday–Week 3

Cats

Raymond has a pet cat. His cat eats 5 ounces of cat food each day. How many ounces of cat food will Raymond's cat eat in one week?

Name:

Work Space:

Answer:

_____ ounces

Daily Word Problems

Tuesday–Week 3

Cats

Raymond's cat eats 1 can of cat food each day. Each can of cat food costs 50¢. How much money will Raymond spend on cat food in one week?

Name:

Work Space:

Answer:

$_____

Daily Word Problems

Wednesday–Week 3

Cats

Raymond's cat had 6 kittens. He wants to sell the kittens for $4.00 each. How much money would he earn if he sells all the kittens?

Name:

Work Space:

Answer:

$ _____

Daily Word Problems

Thursday–Week 3

Cats

Raymond's cat sleeps 16 hours every day. How many hours is Raymond's cat awake each day?

Name:

Work Space:

Answer:

_____ hours

Daily Word Problems

Friday-Week 3

Cats

| A | B | C | D | E | F |

Janice wants to buy two kittens from Raymond. Janice is not sure which two cats she wants to buy. She started to list all the different combinations of 2 cats that she could buy. Complete her list.

A and B   A and C

_____

_____

• How many different combinations are there?   _____

Daily Word Problems

Monday-Week 4

Bicycle

Samantha wants to buy a two-wheel bicycle. The bike costs $55.00. She has saved $33.00. How much more money does she need to save to buy the bike?

Name:

Work Space:

Answer:

$ _____

Daily Word Problems

Tuesday-Week 4

Bicycle

After saving for another month, Samantha needs $16.00 more to buy a bicycle. Her mom will pay her $2.00 an hour for pulling weeds in the yard. How many hours of weed pulling will Samantha need to do to earn $16.00?

Name:

Work Space:

Answer:

_____ hours

Daily Word Problems

Wednesday-Week 4

Bicycle

Samantha's mom bought her a helmet for $25.00, bicycling gloves for $16.00, and an inner tube repair kit for $5.00. How much did Samantha's mom spend in all?

Name:

Work Space:

Answer:

$ _____

Daily Word Problems

Thursday-Week 4

Bicycle

Samantha rode her new bike around the block 16 times. She traveled ½ mile each time she went around the block. How many miles did she travel in all?

Name:

Work Space:

Answer:

_____ miles

Daily Word Problems

Name: _____

Bicycle

Samantha rode her bike every day for a week. She kept a log of how far she rode her bicycle each day.

Sunday	2 miles
Monday	1 mile
Tuesday	1 mile
Wednesday	2 miles
Thursday	3 miles
Friday	2 miles
Saturday	4 miles

Use the log to answer the following questions.

• How far did she ride in one week? _____

• If she continues to ride the same number of miles each week, how many miles in all will she ride in two weeks? _____

In three weeks? _____

In four weeks? _____

• Challenge: How many miles will she ride in one year? (Hint: There are 52 weeks in a year.) _____

Daily Word Problems

Monday-Week 5

Zoo Visit

Dan went to the zoo with his mom, his 11-year-old brother, and his 7-year-old sister. The admission to the zoo was $7.00 for adults and $3.00 for children. How much was the admission for the family?

Name:

Work Space:

Answer:

$ _____

Daily Word Problems

Tuesday-Week 5

Zoo Visit

Dan's brother likes to count all the legs of the animals in a pen. He counted 32 buffalo legs. How many buffalo were in the pen?

Name:

Work Space:

Answer:

_____ buffalo

Daily Word Problems

Wednesday-Week 5

Zoo Visit

According to the sign, the adult giraffe is 18 feet tall. A zookeeper told Dan that the young giraffe is half as tall as her mom. How tall is the young giraffe?

Name:

Work Space:

Answer:

_____ feet tall

Daily Word Problems

Thursday-Week 5

Zoo Visit

The oldest zoo in the United States is the Central Park Zoo in New York City. The zoo opened in 1864.

1. How many years had the Central Park Zoo been open in 1964?

2. How many years had it been open in the year 2000?

Name:

Work Space:

Answer:

1. _____ years open in 1964

2. _____ years open in 2000

Name:

Zoo Visit

Dan enjoys watching the zookeepers feed the animals. The feeding schedule for some of the zoo animals is given below. Design a schedule for Dan so that he can see as many animals being fed as possible.

Remember:

• He wants to see each animal being fed for the full time.

• He can **not** see more than one animal at a time.

Penguins	9:00 to 9:30 a.m.
Seals	9:15 to 9:30 a.m.
Tigers	10:00 to 10:30 a.m.
Lions	10:00 to 10:30 a.m.
Bears	10:30 to 10:45 a.m.
Hippopotamus	10:30 to 11:00 a.m.
Elephants	10:45 to 11:00 a.m.
Monkeys	11:00 to 11:30 a.m.
Apes	11:00 to 11:15 a.m.
Anteaters	11:15 to 11:30 a.m.

_____

_____

_____

_____

Daily Word Problems

Monday-Week 6

Music

Ann is learning to play the trumpet. She practices 30 minutes every day.

1. How many minutes does she practice in 6 days?

2. How many hours is that?

Name:

Work Space:

Answer:

1. _____ minutes in 6 days

2. _____ hours in 6 days

Daily Word Problems

Tuesday-Week 6

Music

Greg sings in the high school choir. The choir has 12 sopranos, 14 altos, 8 tenors, and 10 basses. How many students sing in the choir?

Name:

Work Space:

Answer:

_____ students

Daily Word Problems

Wednesday-Week 6

Music

Name:

Work Space:

The band director wants to know how long the concert will last. The first song is 7 minutes. The second song is 11 minutes. The third song is 6 minutes. The last song is 13 minutes. The director must also add 2 minutes between songs. How long will the concert last?

Answer:

_____ minutes

Daily Word Problems

Thursday-Week 6

Music

Name:

Work Space:

Andy needs to buy reeds for his clarinet. Each reed costs $2.00. He bought 10 reeds.

1. How much did the reeds cost?

2. What happened to the decimal point in the $2.00 when you multiplied it by 10?

Answer:

1. $_____

2. _____

_____

Daily Word Problems

Friday-Week 6

Name:

Adria is in the school marching band. She knows that the band has 7 people in each column and 10 people in each row.

- How many people are in the band? _____

- There is one row of flute players.
  How many flute players are there? _____

- There are two rows of trombone players.
  How many trombone players are there? _____

- There is one row of drummers.
  How many drummers are there? _____

- There are three rows of trumpet players.
  How many trumpet players are there? _____

Daily Word Problems

Monday-Week 7

Bracelet Making

Jasmine is making bead bracelets for her 3 friends. Jasmine needs 18 beads to make one bracelet. She has 46 beads. Does she have enough beads to make all three bracelets? Explain why she does or doesn't have enough beads.

Name:

Work Space:

18 = 1 Bracelet

46 = ☐ Bracelet

$$\begin{array}{r} 18 \\ + 18 \\ \hline 18 \\ \hline 54 \end{array}$$

Answer: she dosn't have enough because 3 18 equals 54 but she needs 54 to make 3 bracelet not 46.

Daily Word Problems

Tuesday-Week 7

Bracelet Making

Jasmine began selling her bracelets. She has sold 8 so far. She sells each bracelet for $4.00. How much money has she earned?

Name:

Work Space:

$4.00 $4.00 $4.00 $4.00

$4.00 $4.00 $4.00 $4.00

Answer:

$ 32.00

Daily Word Problems

Wednesday-Week 7

Bracelet Making

Jasmine wants to know how much money she has spent on materials to make the bracelets. The materials for each bracelet cost $2.00. How much has she spent on the materials for 8 bracelets?

Name:

Work Space:

Answer:

$_____

Daily Word Problems

Thursday-Week 7

Bracelet Making

Jasmine spent $20.00 on materials to make bracelets. She sold 10 bracelets for $3.00 each. Write a number sentence that shows how much money Jasmine made after the cost of the materials.

Name:

Work Space:

Answer:

_____

Daily Word Problems

Name:

Bracelet Making

Jasmine needs your help in making bracelets. She has started a pattern of beads on the bracelets below. She wants you to continue the pattern of beads for each bracelet.

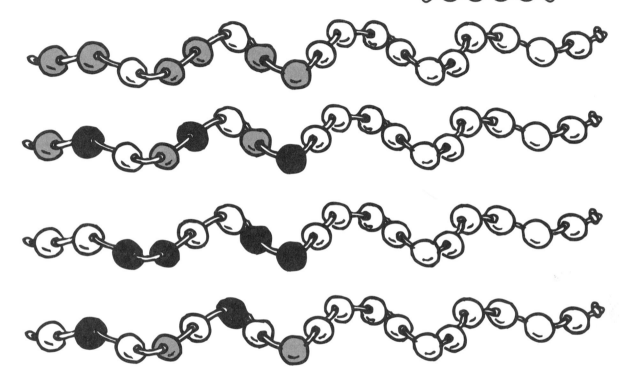

Make your own pattern.

Daily Word Problems

Monday-Week 8

Seashells

Maria has more seashells than Ernie. Ernie has more seashells than Jan.

1. Who has the most seashells?

2. Who has the fewest seashells?

Name:

Work Space:

Answer:

1. _____ has the most seashells

2. _____ has the fewest seashells

Daily Word Problems

Tuesday-Week 8

Seashells

Jesse found one seashell on the beach every 10 minutes.

1. How many seashells did he find in 2 hours?

2. How many did he find in 5 hours?

Name:

Work Space:

Answer:

1. _____ seashells in 2 hours

2. _____ seashells in 5 hours

Daily Word Problems

Wednesday-Week 8

Seashells

Maria is proud of her seashell collection. She has 9 boxes of seashells. The first box has 1 seashell in it. The second has 2 seashells in it, the third has 3, and so on. How many seashells does Maria have in all 9 boxes?

Name:

Work Space:

Answer:

_____ seashells in all

Daily Word Problems

Thursday-Week 8

Seashells

Maria also has a collection of sand dollars. She has five stacks of sand dollars. Each stack has 5 sand dollars in it. How many sand dollars does she have in all?

Name:

Work Space:

Answer:

_____ sand dollars in all

Daily Word Problems

Friday-Week 8

Name:

Seashells

Ernie had 20 small seashells and Maria had 20 large seashells. Ernie traded some of his seashells with Maria. Ernie gave Maria two small seashells for one of her big seashells. They traded a total of 7 times.

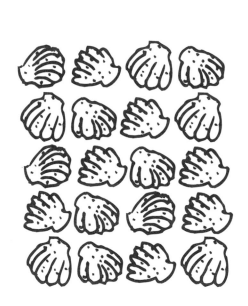

Ernie's Seashells

Maria's Seashells

- How many seashells did Maria get from Ernie? _____
- How many seashells did Ernie get from Maria? _____
- How many seashells did Maria have after trading with Ernie? _____
- How many seashells did Ernie have after trading with Maria? _____

Daily Word Problems

Monday-Week 9

Camping

Ron went camping with his dad. Ron can set up the tent in 12 minutes. His dad can set up the tent in 8 minutes. How much longer does it take Ron to set up the tent?

Name:

Work Space:

Answer:

_____ minutes longer

Daily Word Problems

Tuesday-Week 9

Camping

Ron and his dad went on a hike. The hike started at 7 a.m. They hiked for 4 hours. What time was it when they finished their hike?

Name:

Work Space:

Answer:

_____

Daily Word Problems

Wednesday-Week 9

Camping

Ron and his dad went on another hike. This hike started at 10:30 a.m. and finished at 3 p.m. How many hours did they hike?

Name:

Work Space:

Answer:

_____ hours

Daily Word Problems

Thursday-Week 9

Camping

Ron caught a rainbow trout. It was 16 inches long. Ron's dad caught a rainbow trout that was 9 inches long. How much longer was Ron's fish than his dad's fish?

Name:

Work Space:

Answer:

_____ inches longer

Daily Word Problems

Name: _____

Camping

Ron and his dad had a fishing contest. They wanted to see whose fish weighed the most. The charts show how much each fish weighed.

Ron's Fish

Fish	Weight (in pounds)
1st	2
2nd	1
3rd	$2\frac{1}{2}$
4th	$1\frac{1}{2}$
5th	2

Ron's Dad's Fish

Fish	Weight (in pounds)
1st	1
2nd	$1\frac{1}{2}$
3rd	$\frac{1}{2}$
4th	2
5th	$\frac{1}{2}$
6th	1

• Who won the contest? Explain why.

_____

_____

_____

Daily Word Problems

Monday-Week 10

Snow

Rachel looked out her window and saw snow falling. After one hour she measured the depth of the snow. It was $1\frac{1}{2}$ inches deep. If the snow continues to fall at the same rate, how deep will the snow be after three hours?

Name:

Work Space:

Answer:

_____ inches deep

Daily Word Problems

Tuesday-Week 10

Snow

Rachel made a snowman. The snowman was made from 3 large balls of snow. The first ball was 30 inches tall, the second ball was 23 inches tall, and the third ball was 17 inches tall. How tall was the snowman when all 3 balls of snow were stacked on top of each other?

Name:

Work Space:

Answer:

_____ inches tall

Daily Word Problems
Wednesday-Week 10

Snow

Rachel decided to earn money by shoveling snow off her neighbors' sidewalks. She charged $3.00 a sidewalk. She shoveled 7 sidewalks. How much money did she earn?

Name:

Work Space:

Answer:

$ _____

Daily Word Problems
Thursday-Week 10

Snow

Rachel took 15 minutes to shovel each sidewalk. How long did she work to shovel all 7 sidewalks? Give your answer in hours and minutes.

Name:

Work Space:

Answer:

_____ hour _____ minutes

Daily Word Problems

Friday–Week 10

Name:

Snow

Rachel kept track of how many sidewalks she shoveled in one week.

Sunday	////
Monday	///
Tuesday	//
Wednesday	/
Thursday	//
Friday	///
Saturday	///// /

Complete the bar graph below to show how many sidewalks Rachel shoveled each day.

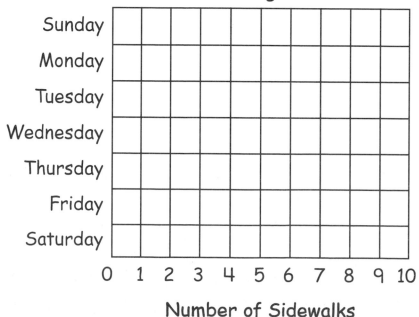

Shoveling Snow

Sunday
Monday
Tuesday
Wednesday
Thursday
Friday
Saturday

0 1 2 3 4 5 6 7 8 9 10

Number of Sidewalks

Daily Word Problems

Monday-Week 11

Bird Feeder

C.J. has a bird feeder. He puts 10 ounces of seed in the feeder each day. How much seed will he use in a week?

Name:

Work Space:

Answer:

_____ ounces of seed in a week

Daily Word Problems

Tuesday-Week 11

Bird Feeder

C.J. bought a bag of birdseed for $4.25. He paid with a $5.00 bill. How much change did he get back?

Name:

Work Space:

Answer:

$_____

Daily Word Problems

Wednesday-Week 11

Bird Feeder

C.J. has 2 bags of birdseed. Each bag holds 90 ounces. If he puts 10 ounces of seed in the feeder each day, how many days can C.J. fill his feeder?

Name:

Work Space:

Answer:

_____ days

Daily Word Problems

Thursday-Week 11

Bird Feeder

Four finches came to C.J.'s bird feeder on Thursday. Twice as many sparrows came as finches. Half as many chickadees came as finches.

1. How many sparrows came to the bird feeder?

2. How many chickadees came?

3. How many birds came in all?

Name:

Work Space:

Answer:

1. _____ sparrows

2. _____ chickadees

3. _____ birds in all

Bird Feeder

C.J. kept a log of the birds that visited his bird feeder.

Sparrows	4
Chickadees	2
Finches	8
Starlings	2

Make a circle graph of the birds at C.J.'s bird feeder. Use a different color for each type of bird.

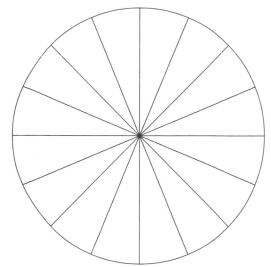

• Half of all the birds that came to the feeder were _____.

• One-fourth of the birds that came to the feeder were _____.

• What fraction of the birds were Chickadees? _____.

Daily Word Problems

Monday–Week 12

Cooking

Name: _____

Work Space:

Miguel wants to make cookies for his class. His recipe makes a batch of 12 cookies. There are 27 students in his class.

1. If the students and his teacher each have one cookie, how many batches of cookies should Miguel make?

2. How many cookies will be left over?

Answer:

1. _____ batches

2. _____ cookies left over

Daily Word Problems

Tuesday–Week 12

Cooking

Name: _____

Work Space:

Mary is making lemonade for lunch. There are 5 people having lunch. Each person's glass holds 9 ounces. A can of lemonade makes 32 ounces. Will Mary have enough lemonade for everyone? Explain why or why not.

Answer: _____

_____

_____

_____

Daily Word Problems

Wednesday-Week 12

Cooking

Jeff made a cake for dessert. The cake measured 10 inches by 10 inches. The cake was cut into 4 pieces that were the same size. What could be the size of each piece?

Name:

Work Space:

10 inches

10 inches

Answer:

_____

Daily Word Problems

Thursday-Week 12

Cooking

Dawn made 22 chewy nut squares. She wants to eat 3 squares a day.

1. How many days will she be able to eat 3 nut squares?

2. How many nut squares will be left over?

Name:

Work Space:

Answer:

1. _____ days

2. _____ nut squares left over

Name:

Cooking

Jenny is a careful shopper. She always looks for the best value on food. She made this list of prices.

	National Brands	Store Brands
Cereal	$3.75	$3.50
Milk	$3.00	$1.75
Bread	$2.25	$2.00
Sugar	$1.50	$1.25
Orange Juice	$2.75	$2.50

• How much will Jenny save in all if she buys the store brands instead of the national brands? $_____

Daily Word Problems

Monday-Week 13

Car Trips

Leta wants to know how far it is to her grandmother's house. A map shows there are 60 miles on the first road, 23 miles on the second road, and 37 miles on the last road to her house. How many miles in all are there to Leta's grandmother's house?

Name:

Work Space:

Answer:

_____ miles

Daily Word Problems

Tuesday-Week 13

Car Trips

Leta's uncle is coming to visit. He plans to make the trip in 3 hours. If the distance is 180 miles, how many miles will he travel each hour?

Name:

Work Space:

Answer:

_____ miles

Daily Word Problems

Wednesday-Week 13

Car Trips

Leta's mother drove for 4 hours to visit her friend. She drove 40 miles each hour. How many miles did Leta's mother travel to her friend's house?

Name:

Work Space:

Answer:

_____ miles

Daily Word Problems

Thursday-Week 13

Car Trips

Leta's motor home gets only 9 miles on each gallon of gas. How many gallons of gas will the motor home use on a trip that is 135 miles long?

Name:

Work Space:

Answer:

_____ gallons

Daily Word Problems

Friday-Week 13

Car Trips

Leta and her mom went on a vacation. Use Leta's travel diary to fill in the missing distances on the map below.

Travel Diary

Day	Distance	Notes
Friday	45 miles	We left home at 10 a.m. and drove through Big City to get to Seaside.
Saturday	40 miles	We ate lunch in Strawberry Fields and then drove to Green River.
Sunday	55 miles	We stopped in Happy Valley to take pictures and then drove home.

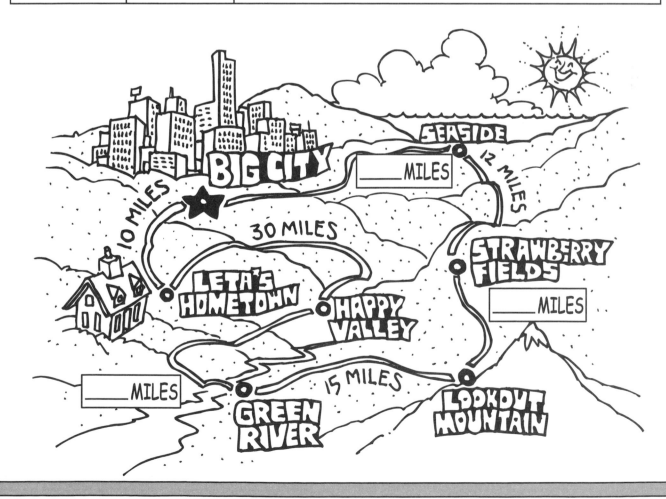

Daily Word Problems

Monday-Week 14

Marbles

Elaine enjoys collecting marbles. She has 292 marbles in her collection. Her display case can hold up to 400 marbles. How many more marbles can she fit in her display case?

Name:

Work Space:

Answer:

_____ more marbles

Daily Word Problems

Tuesday-Week 14

Marbles

Elaine will trade one shooter for 3 cat's-eye marbles. Elaine gave Mark 6 of her shooters. How many cat's-eye marbles should Mark give Elaine?

Name:

Work Space:

Answer:

_____ cat's-eye marbles

Daily Word Problems

Wednesday-Week 14

Marbles

Name: _____

Work Space:

Elaine is a good marbles player. On average, she can shoot 3 marbles out of the circle each round.

1. About how many marbles would she shoot out after 3 rounds?

2. About how many marbles after 4 rounds?

Answer:

1. _____ marbles after 3 rounds

2. _____ marbles after 4 rounds

Daily Word Problems

Thursday-Week 14

Marbles

Name: _____

Work Space:

Elaine was in a marble tournament. The table below shows the number of marbles she knocked out of the circle.

Game	1	2	3	4	5
Number of Marbles	13	11	9	15	7

How many marbles did she knock out of the circle by the end of game 5?

Answer:

_____ marbles

Daily Word Problems

Name:

Marbles

Elaine and Mark played a game of marbles. They each put 10 marbles in the circle.

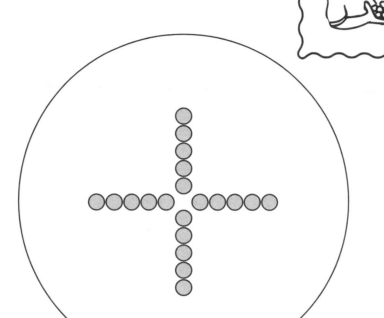

In the first round, Elaine knocked out 3 marbles and Mark knocked out 2 marbles.

In the second round, Elaine knocked out 1 marble and Mark knocked out 2 marbles.

In the third round, Elaine knocked out 4 marbles and Mark knocked out 3 marbles.

• How many marbles in all did Elaine knock out? _____

• How many marbles in all did Mark knock out? _____

• How many marbles were left in the circle for the fourth round? _____

Daily Word Problems

Monday-Week 15

Building Blocks

Erich has a set of building blocks. There are 240 blocks in the set. Conrad asked Erich if he could play with half of the blocks. How many blocks should Erich give to Conrad?

Name:

Work Space:

Answer:

_____ blocks

Daily Word Problems

Tuesday-Week 15

Building Blocks

Erich was stacking his blocks. The bottom row had 6 blocks. Each new row had one less block than the row before. The top row had only one block. How many blocks did he use in all?

Name:

Work Space:

Answer:

_____ blocks in all

 Daily Word Problems • EMC 3003

Daily Word Problems

Wednesday-Week 15

Building Blocks

Conrad wants to make a house out of the blocks. He has 148 blocks. Each wall of his house needs 30 blocks. The roof needs 20 blocks. If the house has 4 walls, will he have enough blocks to make the house? Explain why or why not.

Name:

Work Space:

Answer: _____

_____

_____

_____

Daily Word Problems

Thursday-Week 15

Building Blocks

Erich is making a 5-story building. Each story needs 70 blocks.

1. How many blocks will Erich need to make the building?

2. How many blocks will Erich need to make a 10-story building?

Name:

Work Space:

Answer:

1. _____ blocks for a 5-story building

2. _____ blocks for a 10-story building

Name:

Building Blocks

You may remember that Erich has 240 blocks in his set. The number of blocks he needs to make several projects is shown below.

Project	Number of Blocks
House	120
Car	120
Garage	120
Robot	60
Boat	60

Erich wants to know how many different combinations of projects he can make using all his blocks. For example: He can make a house and a car because the blocks he needs for both of those add up to 240 blocks, the exact amount of blocks in the set. What other combinations of projects can you find?

_____

_____

_____

Daily Word Problems

Monday-Week 16

Ice-Cream Party

Mrs. Rock is planning an ice-cream party for her class. She needs one cone for each of her 25 students and one cone for herself. There are 10 ice-cream cones in a box.

1. How many boxes of cones should she buy?

2. How many cones will be left over?

Name:

Work Space:

Answer:

1. _____ boxes of cones

2. _____ cones left over

Daily Word Problems

Tuesday-Week 16

Ice-Cream Party

Mrs. Rock wants to know how much ice cream she will need. She will give each of her 25 students and herself two scoops of ice cream. How many scoops of ice cream will she need?

Name:

Work Space:

Answer:

_____ scoops

Daily Word Problems

Wednesday-Week 16

Ice-Cream Party

More people like chocolate ice cream than rocky road. The same number of people like rocky road and strawberry. More people like strawberry than vanilla.

1. Which flavor of ice cream do the most people like?

2. Which flavor do the fewest people like?

Name:

Work Space:

Answer:

1. most like _____

2. fewest like _____

Daily Word Problems

Thursday-Week 16

Ice-Cream Party

Mrs. Rock went to the store to buy the ice cream. She received 3 coins that equal 36¢ in change. Which coins did she receive?

Name:

Work Space:

Answer:

_____

_____

Ice-Cream Party

Today is the ice-cream party. Each person will get a 2-scoop cone. They can choose from vanilla, chocolate, strawberry, or rocky road ice cream.

Remember, a person can have 2 scoops of the same kind of ice cream, and a chocolate scoop on top of a vanilla scoop is the same as a vanilla scoop on top of chocolate. Two ways are shown below.

• How many different 2-scoop cones can be made?

Daily Word Problems

Monday–Week 17

Statistics

Ms. Sim's class is learning about statistics. Ms. Sim asked her students to choose their favorite color. One-half of the students chose green, one-fourth chose blue, and one-fourth chose red. There are 24 students in Ms. Sim's class. How many students chose each color?

Name:

Work Space:

Answer:

_____ students chose green

_____ students chose blue

_____ students chose red

Daily Word Problems

Tuesday–Week 17

Statistics

Mr. Gross collected data about his students' favorite types of books. He discovered that most students liked mystery books. The fewest number of students liked science fiction. More students liked fantasy books than science fiction books. More students liked nonfiction books than fantasy books. Put the types of books in order from most to fewest liked.

Name:

Work Space:

Answer:

most liked   1. _____

2. _____

3. _____

fewest liked   4. _____

Daily Word Problems

Wednesday-Week 17

Statistics

Mr. Price discovered that 2 of his students liked hot dogs. Four times as many students liked hamburgers as hot dogs. Ten times as many students liked pizza as hot dogs.

1. How many students liked hamburgers?

2. How many liked pizza?

Name: _____

Work Space:

Answer:

1. _____ students liked hamburgers

2. _____ students liked pizza

Daily Word Problems

Thursday-Week 17

Statistics

Ms. Quon discovered that 40 students liked soccer, 20 liked basketball, 10 liked football, and 5 liked swimming.

1. How many times as many students liked basketball as football?

2. Soccer as football?

3. Basketball as swimming?

Name: _____

Work Space:

Answer:

1. _____ times as many students liked basketball

2. _____ times as many students liked soccer

3. _____ times as many students liked basketball

Daily Word Problems

Name: _____

Statistics

Students in Mr. Teal's class discovered that some students' names begin with the same letter.

> Audie, Audra, Austin,
> Cameron, Carlos, Connor,
> Corrina, David, Erich, Heidi, Ian, Jewel, Joey, Joshua, KoKo, Leslie, Laura, Mason, Matthew, Megan, Michael, Miranda, Natalie, Nina, Preston, Reed, Sarah, Samantha, Savanna, Tara, Thomas, Trevor, Vinny

Complete the graph.

Beginning Letter of Students' Names

A	○ ○ ○
C	
D	
E	
H	
I	
J	
K	
L	
M	
N	
P	
R	
S	
T	
V	

• What letter was used to begin the most student names? _____

• How many more students' names begin with the letter S than the letter D? _____

• How many students' names begin with the letter L? _____

• How many students are in Mr. Teal's class? _____

Daily Word Problems

Monday-Week 18

Centimeters

Ms. Metz helped her students estimate the length of objects. Students would estimate a length and then compare it to the real measurement. Dana estimated that the length of her desk was 80 centimeters. The desk measured 65 centimeters. How far off was her estimate?

Name:

Work Space:

Answer:

_____ centimeters off

Daily Word Problems

Tuesday-Week 18

Centimeters

Ms. Metz had her students estimate the length and width of a math book. Dana's estimate was 40 cm by 20 cm. The book measured 24 cm by 16 cm. How far off was her estimate?

Name:

Work Space:

Answer:

_____ cm by _____ cm off

Daily Word Problems

Wednesday-Week 18

Centimeters

Ms. Metz had each student estimate his or her own height. Dana's estimate was 150 cm. Her real height was 115 cm. How far off was her estimate?

Lily's height was 122 cm. How much taller is Lily than Dana?

Name:

Work Space:

Answer:

_____ cm off

_____ cm taller

Daily Word Problems

Thursday-Week 18

Centimeters

Students estimated the length of their class coat rack. Dana estimated 190 cm. The length was really 220 cm. How far off was her estimate?

Dana used her centimeter ruler to measure the coat rack. Her ruler was 20 cm long. How many times did she lay her ruler end to end to measure the coat rack?

Name:

Work Space:

Answer:

_____ cm off

_____ times

Name:

Dana estimated that her VCR was 10 centimeters tall, her television was 50 centimeters tall, and the television stand was 25 centimeters tall. When she measured with a ruler, she found that she was 3 centimeters too short for the VCR, 12 centimeters too long for the television, and 7 centimeters too long for the stand. Write the actual measurements on the lines below.

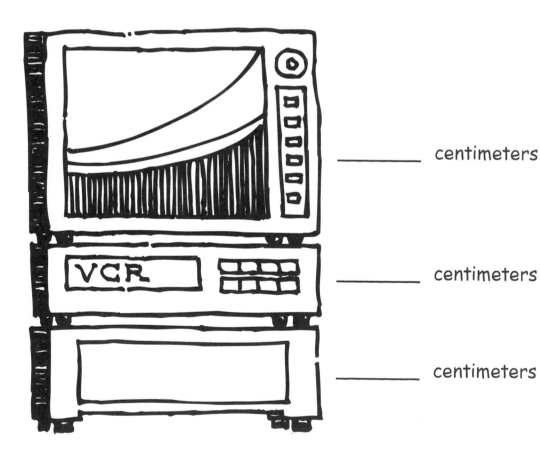

_____ centimeters

_____ centimeters

_____ centimeters

Daily Word Problems

Monday-Week 19

Logic Problems

Sue is taller than Allison, but shorter than Dana. Virginia is the same height as Allison. Mary is taller than Dana. Who is the tallest? Draw pictures to help you find the answer.

Name:

Work Space:

Answer:

_____ is tallest

Daily Word Problems

Tuesday-Week 19

Logic Problems

Guess the mystery number. The number is greater than 10 and less than 18. The number is the sum of two identical odd numbers. What is the number? Show how you found your answer.

Name:

Work Space:

Answer:

_____

Daily Word Problems

Wednesday–Week 19

Logic Problems

Figure out whether James is hiding in the living room, garage, bedroom, kitchen, or basement. Clues: He didn't just cook up a good place to hide. He never takes hiding lying down. He won't need to buckle up where he's hiding. You won't have to dig deep to find him.

Name:

Work Space:

Answer:

James is hiding in the _____ .

Daily Word Problems

Thursday–Week 19

Logic Problems

Guess the mystery number. The number is a multiple of 5. The number is a two-digit number ending in a 5. The number is less than 25.

Name:

Work Space:

Answer:

_____

Daily Word Problems

Friday-Week 19

Logic Problems

Use the clues below to find each boy's favorite color.

When you know that a name and a color do **not** go with each other, make an **X** under the color and across from the name. When you know that a name and color **do** go together, write **YES** in that box. Then you can **X** that name and color for all others.

	Blue	Green	Yellow	Red
Greg				
Ian				
Andy				
Fred				

Clues:

- Each boy has a different color as his favorite.
- Greg and Ian don't like blue.
- Ian and Andy don't like green.
- Greg and Andy don't like yellow.
- Andy, Greg, and Fred don't like red.

Daily Word Problems

Monday–Week 20

Shopping

Shelley and her mom are going shopping downtown. They parked the car in front of a parking meter that takes a quarter for each half hour. Shelley and her mom plan to shop from 1 p.m. to 3:30 p.m.

1. How many quarters will they need to put in the parking meter?

2. How much money will parking cost?

Name:

Work Space:

Answer:

1. _____ quarters

2. $_____

Daily Word Problems

Tuesday–Week 20

Shopping

Shelley's mom bought a pair of shoes for $40.00. The tax on the shoes was 5%. This means for each dollar spent, 5¢ in tax is added.

1. How much did Shelley's mom pay in tax?

2. How much was her total bill?

Name:

Work Space:

Answer:

1. $_____ tax

2. $_____

Daily Word Problems

Wednesday-Week 20

Shopping

Shelley and her mom had a snack while they were shopping. They each had a drink for $1.25 and a soft pretzel for $1.75. What was the total bill for Shelley and her mom?

Name:

Work Space:

Answer:

$ _____

Daily Word Problems

Thursday-Week 20

Shopping

Shelley wanted to buy a goldfish. She bought the goldfish for $0.50, a bowl for $2.00, food for $1.50, and rocks for $0.50. Shelley had $6.00.

1. What was her total bill?

2. How much money did she have left?

Name:

Work Space:

Answer:

1. $ _____

2. $ _____ left

Daily Word Problems

Name:

Shopping

Shelley wanted to buy some clothes that were on sale.

Blouses	Pants	Socks	Shoes
$10	$10	$5	$20
$15	$20	$10	$30
$25	$35	$15	$40

Her mother said she could spend $85. List **all** the different ways that Shelley can buy 1 blouse, 1 pair of pants, 1 pair of socks, and 1 pair of shoes that total **exactly** $85. One way has been done for you.

Blouses	Pants	Socks	Shoes
$10	$20	$15	$40

Daily Word Problems

Monday—Week 21

Money

Pierre's mom will pay him $16.00 if he cleans the garage today. She will cut the amount in half for each day that he waits. Pierre waited 3 days to clean the garage. How much was he paid?

Name:

Work Space:

Answer:

$ _____

Daily Word Problems

Tuesday—Week 21

Money

Pierre and his 3 brothers want to buy a gift for their mom. They want to equally share the cost of the gift. The gift costs $24.00. How much should each brother pay?

Name:

Work Space:

Answer:

$ _____ each

Daily Word Problems

Wednesday-Week 21

Money

Pierre was paid $8.00 each time he mowed the lawn. By the end of the summer he had mowed the lawn 20 times. He saved all the money. How much money did Pierre save?

Name:

Work Space:

Answer:

$ _____

Daily Word Problems

Thursday-Week 21

Money

Pierre wants to buy a pair of rollerblades for $90.00. His dad said he would loan Pierre the money if he pays him 6 dollars a week. How many weeks will Pierre have to pay his dad?

Name:

Work Space:

Answer:

_____ weeks

Money

Pierre wants to exchange a quarter for pennies, nickels, and dimes. List all the different ways to exchange a quarter for other coins. The first one has been done for you.

Pennies	Nickels	Dimes
25	0	0

• How many ways are there? _____

Daily Word Problems
Monday-Week 22

Science Lab

Suki wants to pour 25 milliliters of water, 35 milliliters of oil, and 45 milliliters of syrup into the same beaker for a science experiment. The beaker holds up to 100 milliliters. Will the beaker hold all three liquids? Explain why or why not.

Name:

Work Space:

Answer: _____

_____

_____

_____

Daily Word Problems
Tuesday-Week 22

Science Lab

Ms. Brown held up two beakers to show the class. Each beaker contained 30 milliliters of liquid. She poured the liquids together. A reaction occurred, causing a gas to escape. Only 40 milliliters of the liquid remained. How much of the liquid turned into a gas?

Name:

Work Space:

Answer:

_____ milliliters

Daily Word Problems

Wednesday-Week 22

Science Lab

Suki poured some salt into a beaker on the scale. The salt and beaker together weighed 205 grams. If an empty beaker weighs 25 grams, how much did the salt weigh?

Name:

Work Space:

Answer:

_____ grams

Daily Word Problems

Thursday-Week 22

Science Lab

Suki was in her class's model bridge-building contest. She put the following weights on her bridge before it broke:
three 500-gram weights,
two 250-gram weights,
six 100-gram weights, and
one 50-gram weight. How much weight did Suki's bridge hold before it broke?

Name:

Work Space:

Answer:

_____ grams

Daily Word Problems

Name: _____

Science Lab

Suki was learning about evaporation. She put a dish of water in the shade and an identical dish of water in the sun. She checked the water level every half hour.

Amount of Water Left in the Dish

Time	Dish in the Sun	Dish in the Shade
10:00 a.m.	350 mL	350 mL
10:30 a.m.	275 mL	300 mL
11:00 a.m.	175 mL	250 mL
11:30 a.m.	100 mL	225 mL
12:00 noon	50 mL	200 mL
12:30 p.m.	0 mL	150 mL
1:00 p.m.		125 mL
1:30 p.m.		75 mL
2:00 p.m.		50 mL
2:30 p.m.		25 mL
3:00 p.m.		0 mL

Use the chart to answer the following questions.

• How much longer did it take for all the water to evaporate from the dish in the shade than from the dish in the sun?

_____

• How much water evaporated the first hour from the dish in the sun?

_____

• How much water evaporated the last hour from the dish in the shade?

_____

• Predict how long it would take 500 mL of water to evaporate from a dish in the sun.

_____

Daily Word Problems

Monday-Week 23

Temperature

Dave looked at his outdoor thermometer in the morning. The temperature was 35°. In the afternoon the temperature was 42°. How much warmer was it in the afternoon than in the morning?

Name:

Work Space:

Answer:

°
_____ warmer

Daily Word Problems

Tuesday-Week 23

Temperature

The weatherman reported that the high temperature for the day was 15° higher than the low temperature. If the high temperature was 61°, what was the low temperature?

Name:

Work Space:

Answer:

°
_____

Daily Word Problems
Wednesday-Week 23

Temperature

Dave's normal body temperature is 98°. Today he is not feeling well and has a temperature of 102°. How much did his temperature rise?

Name:

Work Space:

Answer:

°
_____

Daily Word Problems
Thursday-Week 23

Temperature

Dave has a temperature of 102°. His mother gave him some medicine. The medicine brought his temperature down to 99°. How much did his temperature drop?

Name:

Work Space:

Answer:

°
_____

Name:

Temperature

The graph shows the highest daily outdoor temperatures for one week.

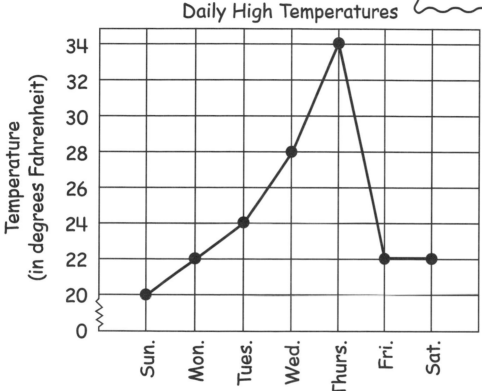

Daily High Temperatures

Temperature (in degrees Fahrenheit)

Day of the Week

Use the graph to answer the following questions.

• Which day had the highest temperature? _____

• Which day had the lowest temperature? _____

• Between which two days did the temperature rise the most?

_____ _____

• On which two days did the temperature remain the same?

_____ _____

Daily Word Problems

Monday-Week 24

Making A Mosaic Table

Alice is making a mosaic table. She needs to buy 144 square tiles. Each tile costs 8¢. How much will all the tiles cost?

Name:

Work Space:

Answer:

$ _____

Daily Word Problems

Tuesday-Week 24

Making A Mosaic Table

Alice plans to use a square piece of plywood for the tabletop. She wants to put 12 tiles on each outside edge of the tabletop. Each tile measures 2 inches by 2 inches. What will be the length of each outside edge of the tabletop?

Name:

Work Space:

Answer:

_____ inches

Daily Word Problems

Wednesday-Week 24

Making A Mosaic Table

Alice bought 4 table legs and 1 jar of cement for her table. Each table leg cost $5.50 and the jar of cement cost $8.25. How much did Alice spend?

Name:

Work Space:

Answer:

$ _____

Daily Word Problems

Thursday-Week 24

Making A Mosaic Table

Alice cemented all the tiles onto the plywood table top. The directions said she must let the cement dry for 48 hours before using it. She finished the table at 2:00 p.m. on Monday. On what day and at what time will the table be ready to use?

Name:

Work Space:

Answer:

_____

_____ : _____

Name:

The design for Alice's mosaic tabletop is shown below. Draw **all** the lines of symmetry on her design.

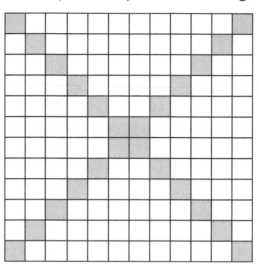

In the grid below, make a different design that has the **same** number of lines of symmetry as Alice's design.

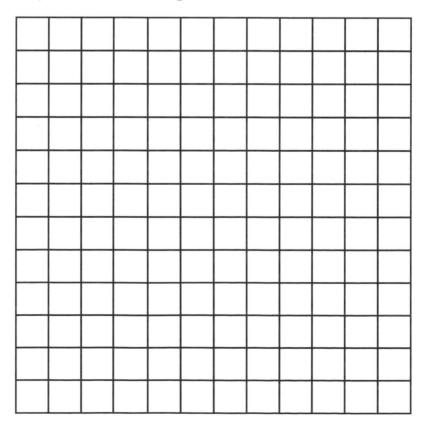

Daily Word Problems

Monday-Week 25

Newspaper Route

Manuel is starting his first newspaper route. He will deliver 17 newspapers. A newspaper subscription costs each customer $6.00 each month. How much will all the customers pay for one month?

Name:

Work Space:

Answer:

$ _____

Daily Word Problems

Tuesday-Week 25

Newspaper Route

Manuel will earn 10¢ for each newspaper he delivers. He delivers 17 newspapers each day.

1. How much money will he earn each day?

2. How much will he earn each week?

Name:

Work Space:

Answer:

1. $ _____ each day

2. $ _____ each week

Daily Word Problems

Wednesday-Week 25

Newspaper Route

Manuel needs rubber bands for the newspapers. He delivers 17 newspapers each day. A box of rubber bands lasts him 9 days. How many rubber bands are in the box?

Name:

Work Space:

Answer:

_____ rubber bands

Daily Word Problems

Thursday-Week 25

Newspaper Route

Manuel would like to ride a bicycle to deliver newspapers. His brother said he would sell Manuel his old bike for $40.00. Manuel said he could pay him $7 a month.

1. How many months will Manuel need to pay for the bike?

2. How much will he pay on the last month?

Name:

Work Space:

Answer:

1. _____ months

2. $_____ on the last month

Name:

Newspaper Route

Manuel made a map to show how many newspapers he delivers on each street. Each rectangle is a block. Each 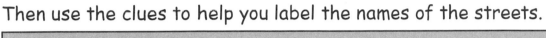 shows where a newspaper should be delivered. Count the number of newspapers delivered on each street. Remember to count **both** sides of each street. Then use the clues to help you label the names of the streets.

Clues:

1. Manuel delivers an odd number of newspapers on Apple Street.

2. He delivers 4 more newspapers on Pear Street than on Peach Street.

3. He delivers 1 more paper on Apple Street than on Cherry Street.

_____ newspapers   _____ Street

_____ newspapers   _____ Street

_____ newspapers   _____ Street

_____ newspapers   _____ Street

Daily Word Problems

Monday-Week 26

Flea Feats

Welcome to flea track-and-field. One of the most popular flea feats is the dog hair high jump. The record is 37 mm.

1. Fred Flea jumped 29 mm. By how much did he miss the record?

2. Frances Flea jumped 41 mm. By how much did she beat the record?

Name:

Work Space:

Answer:

1. _____ mm

2. _____ mm

Daily Word Problems

Tuesday-Week 26

Flea Feats

The record for staying on a wagging dog's tail before falling off is 1 minute 40 seconds. Today Frank Flea beat the record by 27 seconds. What is the new record?

Name:

Work Space:

Answer:

_____ minute _____ seconds

Daily Word Problems

Wednesday-Week 26

Flea Feats

The record for jumping from one dog's ear to the other is 94 mm.

1. Flo Flea jumped 87 mm. Flo missed the record by how many mm?

2. Flynn Flea jumped 93 mm. Sadly, he did not beat the record. But how much farther did he jump than Flo?

Name:

Work Space:

Answer:

1. _____ mm

2. _____ mm farther

Daily Word Problems

Thursday-Week 26

Flea Feats

The Flea Flee is a race from a dog's nose to its tail. Flint Flea's time was 2 minutes and 45 seconds. The record was 3 minutes and 13 seconds. By how much did Flint beat the record?

Name:

Work Space:

Answer:

_____ seconds

Daily Word Problems

Friday-Week 26

Name:

Flea Feats

Finley Flea was a fierce competitor. He could lift dog hairs better than anyone. The bar graph shows his best daily lifts.

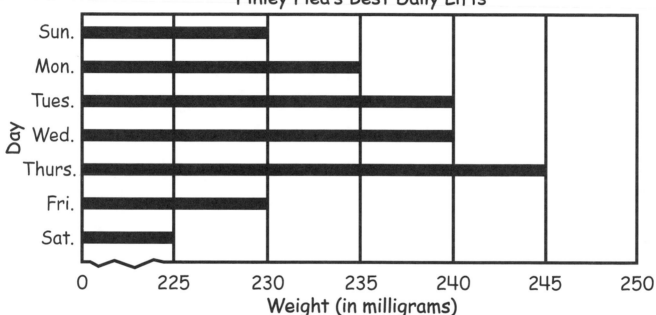

Finley Flea's Best Daily Lifts

Use the bar graph to answer the following questions.

• What was Finley's best lifting day? _____

• What was Finley's worst lifting day? _____

• How much more did he lift on his best
day than on his worst day? _____

• Does Finley lift better in the middle
of the week or on the weekend? _____

Daily Word Problems

Monday-Week 27

Making a Sandbox

Mrs. O'Dell made this diagram of her backyard.

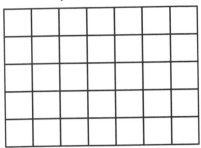

If each square represents 1 square yard, what is the area of her backyard?

Name:

Work Space:

Answer:

_____ square yards

Daily Word Problems

Tuesday-Week 27

Making a Sandbox

Mrs. O'Dell built a wooden fence around her backyard. The yard is 21 feet long by 15 feet wide. What is the total length of the fence?

Name:

Work Space:

Answer:

_____ feet

Daily Word Problems

Wednesday-Week 27

Making a Sandbox

Mrs. O'Dell built a sandbox for her son. The bottom of the sandbox measures 6 feet by 6 feet. The sides are 2 feet high.

1. What shape is the bottom?

2. What shape are the sides?

Name:

Work Space:

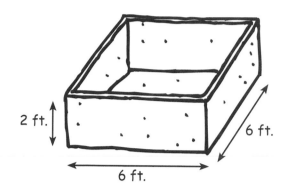

2 ft.

6 ft.

6 ft.

Answer:

1. The bottom is a _____ shape.

2. The sides are a _____ shape.

Daily Word Problems

Thursday-Week 27

Making a Sandbox

Mrs. O'Dell bought some sand for the sandbox. Each bag of sand weighed 50 pounds. She used 7 bags of sand. How much did all of the sand in the sandbox weigh?

Name:

Work Space:

Answer:

_____ pounds

Name: _____

Making a Sandbox

Mrs. O'Dell is taking her son to buy sandbox toys. Her son wants a dump truck, 2 cars, and a pail.

   Dump truck $4.00

   Car $3.50

   Pail $2.50

   Shovel $0.75

- If he can spend up to $15.00, how many shovels can he buy?   _____

Daily Word Problems

Monday-Week 28

Vegetable Gardening

This year the area of Mrs. O'Dell's garden is 72 square feet. Last year she had two small gardens that each measured 18 square feet. How many times larger is this year's garden than last year's gardens combined?

Name:

Work Space:

Answer:

_____ times larger

Daily Word Problems

Tuesday-Week 28

Vegetable Gardening

Mrs. O'Dell has 8 different vegetables to plant in her garden. She wants to divide her garden into 8 squares. Each square should be the same size. Help Mrs. O'Dell divide her garden into 8 squares. What is the measurement of each side of the squares?

Name:

Work Space:

```
        12 feet
   ┌──────────────────┐
   │                  │
6 feet                │
   │                  │
   └──────────────────┘
```

Answer:

_____ by _____

Daily Word Problems • EMC 3003

Daily Word Problems

Wednesday-Week 28

Vegetable Gardening

Name:

Work Space:

Mrs. O'Dell wants to plant 8 different kinds of vegetables in her garden. She wants 8 plants of each kind. Write a number sentence using **addition** that Mrs. O'Dell can use to find the total number of plants she will have in her garden. Write another number sentence that she can use, this time using **multiplication**.

Answer:

addition: _____

multiplication: _____

Daily Word Problems

Thursday-Week 28

Vegetable Gardening

Name:

Work Space:

Sally, Mrs. O'Dell's daughter, pulled weeds in the garden. Sally worked from 8 a.m. to 2 p.m. She took a half hour off for lunch and two 15-minute breaks. How much time did Sally spend pulling weeds?

Answer:

_____ hours

Daily Word Problems

Name:

Vegetable Gardening

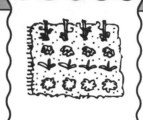

Mrs. O'Dell went to a nursery to buy vegetable plants. Remember that she wants 8 plants of each kind of vegetable. How much did all of the plants cost?

Vegetable Plants	Price for 1 Plant	Price for 8 Plants
onion	.05	
tomato	1.00	
pepper	.50	
broccoli	.75	
potato	.25	
squash	.30	
string bean	.40	
pea	.60	
	TOTAL	

VEGETABLE PLANTS

Daily Word Problems • EMC 3003

Daily Word Problems

Monday—Week 29

Eggs

Kay lives on a farm. Her job is to collect the chicken eggs. On Sunday, Monday, and Friday she collected 15 eggs each day. On Tuesday and Wednesday she collected 14 eggs each day. On Thursday and Saturday she collected 12 eggs each day. How many eggs did she collect during the whole week?

Name:

Work Space:

Answer:

_____ eggs

Daily Word Problems

Tuesday—Week 29

Eggs

Kay puts the eggs in cartons that hold one dozen. Today she has 3 full cartons and another carton that is half full. How many eggs does she have?

Name:

Work Space:

Answer:

_____ eggs

Daily Word Problems

Wednesday-Week 29

Eggs

Kay sells any eggs her family doesn't eat. She collected 105 eggs this week. If her family eats 1½ dozen eggs a week, how many eggs can Kay sell?

Name:

Work Space:

Answer:

_____ eggs

Daily Word Problems

Thursday-Week 29

Eggs

Kay sells eggs for 8¢ each.

1. How much does a dozen eggs cost?

2. How many eggs would you get for $4.00?

Name:

Work Space:

Answer:

1. $_____ for a dozen

2. _____ eggs for $4.00

Daily Word Problems

Friday-Week 29

Eggs

Name:

Kay wanted to know if chickens would lay more eggs if she played music for them. She played music for half of the chickens and no music for the other half. She recorded the number of eggs she collected from each group on the chart below.

Number of Eggs Collected

Day	Music	No Music
1	7	8
2	7	8
3	8	7
4	7	8
5	9	7
6	9	7
7	7	8
8	10	6
9	9	8
10	8	8
11	10	7
12	11	9
13	8	8
14	9	7
15	9	7

• After looking at the chart, decide if the music helped the chickens to lay more eggs or not. Support your decision with information from the chart.

_____

_____

_____

_____

Daily Word Problems

Monday-Week 30

Pizza Fractions

Welcome to Make-Your-Own-Pizza. The pizza dough is all rolled out for you. First, you add the sauce. You need one-half cup of sauce for one pizza.

1. How many pizzas could you make with 1 pint of sauce?

2. How many pizzas could you make with 1 quart of sauce?

Name:

Work Space:

| 2 cups = 1 pint |
| 4 cups = 1 quart |

Answer:

1. _____ pizzas with 1 pint of sauce

2. _____ pizzas with 1 quart of sauce

Daily Word Problems

Tuesday-Week 30

Pizza Fractions

Next, you put on the cheese. You need $\frac{3}{4}$ cup white cheese and $\frac{1}{4}$ cup yellow cheese. Mark how much cheese you'll need in the measuring cups. How much cheese would there be when you put both cheeses together?

Name:

Work Space:

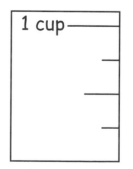

White cheese   Yellow cheese

Answer:

_____

Daily Word Problems

Wednesday-Week 30

Pizza Fractions

Name:

Work Space:

Next, you put on the pepperoni. Pepperoni comes in bags of thin round slices. Each bag contains 100 slices.

1. How many slices of pepperoni would you have on your pizza if you used half the bag?

2. How many slices would you have if you used $\frac{1}{4}$ bag?

Answer:

1. _____ slices using half a bag

2. _____ slices using $\frac{1}{4}$ bag

Daily Word Problems

Thursday-Week 30

Pizza Fractions

Name:

Work Space:

Your pizza needs to bake for 20 minutes at 450 degrees. If you put the pizza in the oven at 11:35 a.m., at what time should you take out the pizza?

Answer:

_____ : _____

Daily Word Problems

Name:

Pizza Fractions

You invite your friends over for pizza. You have 5 pizzas. Each pizza should be divided into equal-sized pieces. Divide pizza A in half, pizza B in thirds, pizza C in fourths, pizza D in sixths, and pizza E in eighths.

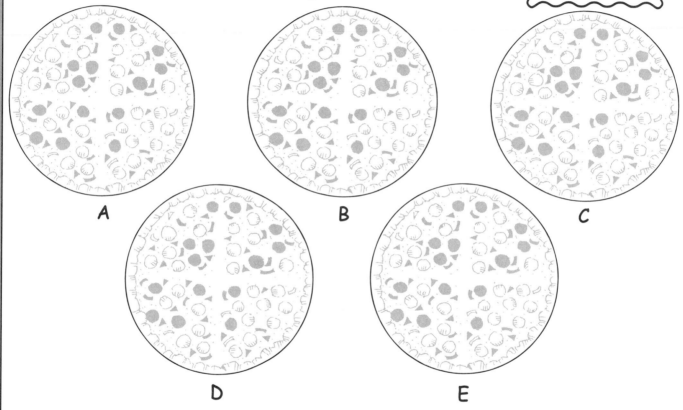

A   B   C

D   E

- Jack and Rob want to eat the same amount of pizza. If Jack eats 3 pieces of pizza C, how many pieces of pizza E should Rob eat? _____

- If Jack eats 2 pieces of pizza B, how many pieces of pizza D should Rob eat? _____

- If Jack eats 1 piece of pizza A, how many pieces of pizza C should Rob eat? _____

Daily Word Problems
Monday-Week 31

Games

Emilio was playing basketball. At halftime, Emilio's team had 32 points and the other team had 28 points. By the end of the game, Emilio's team had doubled their points and won the game by 8 points. What was the final score of the game?

Name:

Work Space:

Answer:

_____ to _____

Daily Word Problems
Tuesday-Week 31

Games

Ben's baseball games have 9 innings. It takes about 20 minutes to play each inning.

1. About how many minutes does it take to play the whole game?

2. How many hours is that?

Name:

Work Space:

Answer:

1. _____ minutes

2. _____ hours

Daily Word Problems

Wednesday-Week 31

Games

Jenna just scored 23,000 points playing her favorite computer game. Her score the last time she played was 19,821 points. How many more points did she score this time than the last time?

Name:

Work Space:

Answer:

_____ more points

Daily Word Problems

Thursday-Week 31

Games

Paula made 2 points in her first basketball game. During the next 3 games, she tripled the number of points she had the game before. How many points did she make in each of those 3 games?

Name:

Work Space:

Answer:

_____ points in the second game

_____ points in the third game

_____ points in the fourth game

Name:

Games

Four friends were playing a computer game. Use the following clues to match each player with his or her best score.

One of the girls had the highest score.

Gary had more points than Heidi and Michael.

Michael had 1,100 more points than Heidi.

Jenna	15,050
Heidi	17,200
Gary	18,000
Michael	16,150

• Who had more points, the boys or the girls? _____

Daily Word Problems

Monday-Week 32

Television

Toby started watching television at 4:00 in the afternoon. He stopped watching at 5:30 p.m. to have dinner.

1. How many hours did Toby watch television?

2. How many minutes?

Name:

Work Space:

Answer:

1. _____ hours

2. _____ minutes

Daily Word Problems

Tuesday-Week 32

Television

If Toby watched 2 hours of television every day, how many hours of television would he watch in a year? (Hint: There are 365 days in a year.)

Name:

Work Space:

Answer:

_____ hours in a year

Daily Word Problems • EMC 3003

Daily Word Problems

Wednesday-Week 32

Television

Toby gets up at 8 a.m. on Saturday mornings. His favorite cartoon show is on at 1:30 in the afternoon. How many hours must Toby wait until his show is on?

Name:

Work Space:

Answer:

_____ hours

Daily Word Problems

Thursday-Week 32

Television

Toby's bedtime is at 9 p.m. on Friday night. He wants to watch a 2½-hour movie that starts at 7 p.m. Will the movie be over before his bedtime? Explain your answer.

Name:

Work Space:

Answer: _____

_____

_____

_____

Daily Word Problems

Name: _____

Television

Toby's parents were worried that he was watching too much television. They asked Toby to keep a log of how much television he watched over a week's time. Here is Toby's log.

Television Log

Day	Number of Minutes
Sunday	120
Monday	30
Tuesday	60
Wednesday	90
Thursday	90
Friday	120
Saturday	90

Use the log to answer the following questions.

• How many minutes of television did Toby watch for the whole week? _____

• How many hours of television did he watch? _____

• If he watches television for the same number of hours each week, how many hours would that be in a year? _____

• On which day or days did he spend the most time watching television? _____

• On which day or days did he spend the least time watching television? _____

• Do you watch more or less television than Toby? _____

Daily Word Problems

Monday-Week 33

Football

A football team scored 2 touchdowns for 6 points each, 1 field goal for 3 points, and a safety for 2 points. How many points did the team score?

Name:

Work Space:

Answer:

_____ points

Daily Word Problems

Tuesday-Week 33

Football

During one football game, the home team scored 14 points in each half of the game. The visitors scored 6 points in each quarter.

1. What was the final score?

2. Who won the game?

Name:

Work Space:

Answer:

1. _____ to _____

2. _____ won

Daily Word Problems • EMC 3003

Daily Word Problems

Wednesday-Week 33

Football

The Tigers gained 14 yards on their first play of the game. On the second play they gained 1 yard, on the third they lost 5 yards, and on the fourth they gained 6 yards. Overall, how many yards did they gain or lose during the first 4 plays?

Name:

Work Space:

Answer:

_____ yards

Daily Word Problems

Thursday-Week 33

Football

A football game started at 10 a.m. The first and second quarters each lasted 9 minutes. There was a break at halftime that lasted 15 minutes. The third quarter lasted 9 minutes. And the fourth quarter lasted 8 minutes. At what time did the game end?

Name:

Work Space:

Answer:

_____ : _____

Daily Word Problems

Name:

Football

Here are some different ways a team can score points in a football game:

- 6 points for a touchdown
- 7 points for a touchdown with an extra point
- 3 points for a field goal
- 2 points for a safety

List **all** the different ways a team could make 9 points. One way has been done for you.

Touchdown 6 points	Touchdown with Extra Point 7 points	Field Goal 3 points	Safety 2 points
1	--	1	--

Daily Word Problems

Monday-Week 34

Jelly Beans

Hugo has 15 green jelly beans. He has twice as many red jelly beans as green, 3 times as many yellow as green, and 20 more orange than green. How many red, yellow, and orange jelly beans does he have?

Name:

Work Space:

Answer:

_____ red jelly beans

_____ yellow jelly beans

_____ orange jelly beans

Daily Word Problems

Tuesday-Week 34

Jelly Beans

Holly wants to buy a bag of jelly beans. The jelly beans cost 75¢ for a quarter of a pound. If Holly buys one pound of jelly beans and gives the clerk $5.00, how much change should she receive?

Name:

Work Space:

Answer:

$_____

Daily Word Problems

Wednesday–Week 34

Jelly Beans

There are 60 jelly beans in a bag. There are 14 pink jelly beans, 18 are purple, 16 are white, and the rest are yellow. If Mindy reaches into the bag without looking and picks one jelly bean, what color is she most likely to pick? What color is she least likely to pick?

Name:

Work Space:

Answer:

Mindy will most likely pick _____.

Mindy will least likely pick _____.

Daily Word Problems

Thursday–Week 34

Jelly Beans

Ryan has 55 jelly beans. He gave 12 to his sister and 15 to his brother. He gave half of the remaining jelly beans to his best friend. How many did he give to his best friend?

Name:

Work Space:

Answer:

_____ jelly beans

Daily Word Problems

Friday-Week 34

Name:

Jelly Beans

Kyle has the following jelly beans:

| 12 red | 24 green | 18 orange |
| 30 pink | 36 yellow | 42 purple |

He wants to share his jelly beans with 6 friends. He wants each person to have the same number of jelly beans and the same number of each color of jelly bean. Help Kyle divide the jelly beans, using the bowls below.

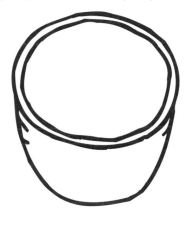 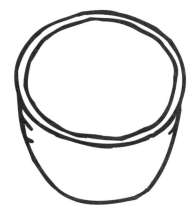 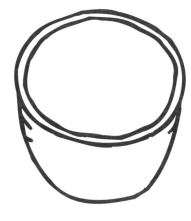

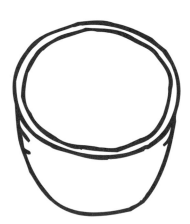 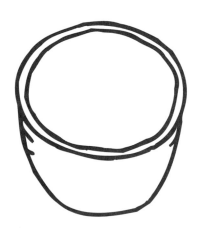 

• How many of each color of jelly bean are in each bowl?

_____ red   _____ green   _____ orange

_____ pink   _____ yellow   _____ purple

• How many jelly beans in all are in each bowl?   _____

Daily Word Problems

Monday–Week 35

Stuffed Animal Collection

Name:

Work Space:

Minna has a stuffed animal collection. She has 21 ocean animals, 5 fewer rainforest animals than ocean animals, and 3 more farm animals than rainforest animals. How many animals does she have in her collection?

Answer:

_____ animals

Daily Word Problems

Tuesday–Week 35

Stuffed Animal Collection

Name:

Work Space:

Last year Minna bought 3 stuffed animals for $4.50 each, 2 stuffed animals for $5.00 each, and 1 for $5.50. How much did she spend on stuffed animals last year?

Answer:

$_____

Daily Word Problems

Wednesday-Week 35

Stuffed Animal Collection

Minna displays her stuffed animal collection in 2 cabinets. In one cabinet, there are 8 large animals on each shelf. In the other cabinet, there are 9 small animals on each shelf. If each cabinet has 7 shelves, how many large and small animals are in each cabinet? How many animals are in both cabinets?

Name:

Work Space:

Answer:

_____ large animals

_____ small animals

_____ animals in all

Daily Word Problems

Thursday-Week 35

Stuffed Animal Collection

Minna has a book that tells how much the stuffed animals are worth. Tim Tiger first sold for $4.50. It was worth 40¢ more each month for the next 6 months. How much is it worth now?

Name:

Work Space:

Answer:

$_____

Daily Word Problems
Friday-Week 35

Stuffed Animal Collection

Minna saw this sign at her favorite store.

Stuffed Animal Collection Store

We want to buy the following stuffed animals!

Andy Antelope
$7.25

Conchetta
Crocodile
$8.00

Bonnie Bear
$5.45

Devin Dog
$6.00

Eddie Eel
$9.90

Minna has all 5 of these animals in her collection. She wants to sell 2 of the animals and use the money she gets to buy some new stuffed animals. The new stuffed animals cost $4.50 each.

• What is the greatest number of new stuffed animals that she could buy?

_____

How much money would be left over?

_____

• What is the fewest number of new stuffed animals that she could buy?

_____

How much money would be left over?

_____

Daily Word Problems

Monday-Week 36

Ocean Depths

Oceans can be deeper than the height of the tallest mountains. In the Pacific Ocean, the Mariana Trench is 35,840 feet deep. The tallest mountain, Mount Everest, is 29,035 feet tall. How much deeper is the Mariana Trench than Mount Everest is tall?

Name:

Work Space:

Answer:

_____ feet deeper

Daily Word Problems

Tuesday-Week 36

Ocean Depths

The average depth of the Indian Ocean is 12,598 feet. The average depth of the Atlantic Ocean is 11,730 feet. How much deeper is the Indian Ocean than the Atlantic Ocean?

Name:

Work Space:

Answer:

_____ feet deeper

Daily Word Problems

Wednesday-Week 36

Ocean Depths

The area of the continent of Antarctica is 5,400,000 square miles. The area of the Arctic Ocean is about 5,105,700 square miles. How much larger is the area of Antarctica than the area of the Arctic Ocean?

Name:

Work Space:

Answer:

_____ square miles larger

Daily Word Problems

Thursday-Week 36

Ocean Depths

The Pacific Ocean is about 64,186,300 square miles in area. The Atlantic Ocean is about 33,420,000 square miles in area. How many square miles are both oceans together?

Name:

Work Space:

Answer:

_____ square miles

Daily Word Problems

Name: _____

Ocean Depths

The chart below shows the size and average depth of the four oceans.

Ocean	Area (in square miles)	Average Depth (in feet)
Arctic	5,105,700	3,407
Atlantic	33,420,000	11,730
Indian	28,350,500	12,598
Pacific	64,186,300	12,925

Use the chart to answer the following questions.

• Put the oceans in order from the largest area to the smallest area.

_____ _____ _____ _____

• What is the difference between the largest area and the smallest area?

_____

• Put the oceans in order from the greatest depth to the smallest depth.

_____ _____ _____ _____

• What is the difference between the greatest depth and the smallest depth?

_____

110

Answer Key

Week 1
Monday—50 minutes
Tuesday—5 candles
Wednesday—55 candles
Thursday—28 inches of wick
Friday—2 faces, 3 stars, 1 bow, 4 flowers;
   Answers will vary: Divide each number by 3.

Week 2
Monday—8:50 a.m.
Tuesday—28 students
Wednesday—16 boys
Thursday—4 gallons
Friday—29 students; stop #2; stop #6; stop #2;
   stop #2; stops #2, #4, and #6; stops #1, #3,
   and #5.

Week 3
Monday—35 ounces
Tuesday—$3.50
Wednesday—$24.00
Thursday—8 hours
Friday—15 combinations—AB, AC, AD, AE, AF, BC,
   BD, BE, BF, CD, CE, CF, DE, DF, EF

Week 4
Monday—$22.00
Tuesday—8 hours
Wednesday—$46.00
Thursday—8 miles
Friday—15 miles; 30 miles; 45 miles; 60 miles;
   780 miles

Week 5
Monday—$16.00
Tuesday—8 buffalo
Wednesday—9 feet tall
Thursday—100 years; 136 years
Friday—Penguins or Seals, Tigers or Lions, Bears,
Elephants, Apes, Anteaters

Week 6
Monday—180 minutes; 3 hours
Tuesday—44 students
Wednesday—43 minutes
Thursday—$20.00; The decimal point moved
   one place to the right.
Friday—70 people; 10 flute players; 20 trombone
   players; 10 drummers; 30 trumpet players

Week 7
Monday—No, she has 46 beads but she needs
   54 beads.
Tuesday—$32.00
Wednesday—$16.00
Thursday—10 x $3.00 - $20.00 = $10.00
Friday—

Student patterns will vary.

Week 8
Monday—Maria has the most; Jan has the fewest
Tuesday—12 seashells; 30 seashells
Wednesday—45 seashells
Thursday—25 sand dollars
Friday—14 seashells; 7 seashells; 27 seashells;
   13 seashells

Week 9
Monday—4 minutes
Tuesday—11 a.m.
Wednesday—4½ hours
Thursday—7 inches
Friday—Ron won because he had 9 pounds of fish.
   Ron's dad only had 6½ pounds of fish.

Week 10
Monday—4½ inches deep
Tuesday—70 inches tall OR 5 feet 10 inches tall
Wednesday—$21.00
Thursday—1 hour 45 minutes
Friday—

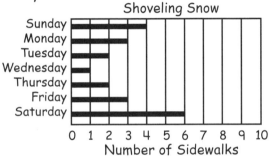

Week 11
Monday—70 ounces of seed
Tuesday—$0.75
Wednesday—18 days
Thursday—8 sparrows; 2 chickadees; 14 birds in all
Friday—Circle graph should show 4 sections for
   Sparrows, 2 for Chickadees, 8 for Finches, and
   2 for Starlings; Finches; Sparrows; ⅛

Week 12
Monday—3 batches; 8 cookies left over
Tuesday—No, the can of lemonade makes 32 ounces
   and she needs 45 ounces.
Wednesday—5 inches by 5 inches OR 2½ inches by
   10 inches
Thursday—7 days; 1 nut square left over
Friday—$2.25

Week 13
Monday—120 miles
Tuesday—60 miles
Wednesday—160 miles
Thursday—15 gallons
Friday—35 miles from Big City to Seaside;
   13 miles from Strawberry Fields to Lookout
   Mountain; 25 miles from Green River to
   Happy Valley.

Week 14
Monday—108 more marbles
Tuesday—18 cat's-eye marbles
Wednesday—9 marbles; 12 marbles
Thursday—55 marbles
Friday—8 marbles; 7 marbles; 5 marbles

Week 15
Monday—120 blocks
Tuesday—21 blocks
Wednesday—Yes, he needs 140 blocks to make a house
    and he has 148.
Thursday—350 blocks; 700 blocks
Friday—House and car; house and garage; car and
    garage; house, robot, and boat; car, robot, and
    boat; garage, robot, and boat

Week 16
Monday—3 boxes, 4 cones left over
Tuesday—52 scoops
Wednesday—most like chocolate; fewest like vanilla
Thursday—1 quarter, 1 dime, and 1 penny
Friday—10 different cones—V=vanilla, C=chocolate,
    S=strawberry, R=rocky road: VV VC VS VR
    CC CS CR SS SR RR

Week 17
Monday—12 chose green, 6 chose blue, 6 chose red
Tuesday—Mystery, nonfiction, fantasy, science fiction
Wednesday—8 liked hamburgers; 20 liked pizza
Thursday—2 times; 4 times; 4 times
Friday—M; 2 more; 2 students' names; 33 students

Week 18
Monday—15 cm off
Tuesday—16 cm by 4 cm off
Wednesday—35 cm off; 7 cm taller
Thursday—30 cm off; 11 times
Friday—13 cm for the VCR; 38 cm for the TV;
    18 cm for the stand

Week 19
Monday—Mary is tallest
Tuesday—14
Wednesday—living room
Thursday—15
Friday—Greg=green, Ian=red, Andy=blue, Fred=yellow

Week 20
Monday—5 quarters; $1.25
Tuesday—$2.00 tax; $42.00
Wednesday—$6.00
Thursday—$4.50; $1.50 left
Friday—
    $10 blouse, $20 pants, $15 socks, $40 shoes;
    $10 blouse, $35 pants, $10 socks, $30 shoes;
    $15 blouse, $20 pants, $10 socks, $40 shoes;
    $15 blouse, $35 pants, $5 socks, $30 shoes;
    $15 blouse, $35 pants, $15 socks, $20 shoes;
    $25 blouse, $10 pants, $10 socks, $40 shoes;
    $25 blouse, $20 pants, $10 socks, $30 shoes;
    $25 blouse, $35 pants, $5 socks, $20 shoes

Week 21
Monday—$2.00
Tuesday—$6.00 each
Wednesday—$160.00
Thursday—15 weeks
Friday—12 ways—25 pennies and 0 nickels and
    0 dimes; 20 pennies and 1 nickel; 15 pennies
    and 2 nickels; 15 pennies and 1 dime; 10 pennies
    and 3 nickels; 10 pennies, 1 nickel, and 1 dime;
    5 pennies and 4 nickels; 5 pennies, 2 nickels, and
    1 dime; 5 pennies and 2 dimes; 1 nickel and 2 dimes;
    3 nickels and 1 dime; 5 nickels

Week 22
Monday—No, there are 105 ml of liquids, which is 5 ml
    more than the beaker will hold.
Tuesday—20 milliliters
Wednesday—180 grams
Thursday—2,650 grams
Friday—2½ hours longer; 175 ml; 50 ml; Answers will
    vary, but should be in the range of 3 to 4 hours.

Week 23
Monday—7° warmer
Tuesday—46°
Wednesday—4°
Thursday—3°
Friday—Thursday; Sunday; between Wednesday and
    Thursday; Friday and Saturday

Week 24
Monday—$11.52
Tuesday—24 inches
Wednesday—$30.25
Thursday—Wednesday 2:00 p.m.
Friday—4 lines of symmetry should be drawn; Student
    designs will vary, but should have 4 lines of
    symmetry.

Week 25
Monday—$102.00
Tuesday—$1.70/day; $11.90/week
Wednesday—153 rubber bands
Thursday—6 months; $5.00 the last month
Friday—5 newspapers on Apple Street; 4 newspapers
    on Cherry Street; 2 newspapers on Peach Street;
    6 newspapers on Pear Street

Week 26
Monday—8 mm; 4 mm
Tuesday—2 minutes 7 seconds
Wednesday—7 mm; 6 mm farther
Thursday—28 seconds
Friday—Thursday; Saturday; 20 milligrams;
    middle of the week

Week 27
Monday—35 square yards
Tuesday—72 feet
Wednesday—square; rectangle
Thursday—350 pounds
Friday—2 shovels